Pickleball Poetry

Fun and Whimsical Verses to Dink About

Always play the soft game...
Best wishes,
Doug Snelson

Written by Doug Snelson
Illustrations by Jim Ditmars

Acknowledgements

I'm extremely grateful to Andrea (Andy) Marcell Jones and Karl Lombel for their pickleball expertise, input, and friendship. Thanks to Jim Ditmars for his creative and fun illustrations, Tony Fradkin for his vision and attention to detail with the design layout, and Diane Phillips Snelson, my wife and publishing teammate, for keeping me out of the non-volley zone as we partnered on and off the court to get this book published.

And thanks, too, to my father, Howard Snelson, for teaching me table tennis and tennis decades before I heard of pickleball. To my siblings, Bob, Brent, and Lois, who did ping pong battles with me in the basement on many rainy summer mornings as kids. And to my mother, Anne Snelson, who always encouraged reading and, especially, my writing at a young age.

Pickleball Poetry: Fun and Whimsical Verses to Dink About
Copyright © 2023 Petalous Publishing, LLC

Published by Petalous Publishing, LLC
PO Box 1332, Bluffton, SC 29910

ISBN: 978-0-9777811-6-4
Printed in the United States of America

First Edition

dougsnelson.com

For my parents
Howard and Anne Snelson

Introduction

A few of my neighbors invited me to play pickleball for the first time about eight years ago. "What's pickleball?" I asked.

Lines for pickleball were installed on the tennis courts in the community where I resided.

In my glory days, ping pong and tennis were mainstays of my athletic activities. I learned how to make a good shot by connecting my paddle or racquet with the ball. However, the plastic pickleball with holes didn't bounce like I was used to hitting. I had to anticipate sooner and reach farther to make contact. In addition, the wooden paddle provided by the community gave off a clicking sound every time I hit the ball.

I banged the ball with success all summer until I played against players who simply reset all my drives until I missed.

I paid attention. Good players showed me how the game should be played. I learned the fundamentals of the soft game. I made new friends.

I bought a paddle, then another. I got better. I watched, observed, applied what I learned, and observed some more. I played in tournaments. "This is so much fun!", I thought.

One afternoon while writing on the beach in Long Beach Island, NJ, I created some whimsical rhymes about pickleball. The rhymes became poems.

I hope this book makes every pickleball player smile.

As in life, always play the soft game, be patient, laugh a lot, and paddle click.

"One day I will find the right words,
and they will be simple." — Jack Kerouac

Table of Contents

Pickled

I play with you, it's 0-0-2,
Confident, true, we are so due,
Our opponents pose us no threat.

I play with verve, a perfect serve,
Yet I observe, my shot will swerve,
Poor follow through has found the net.

We need to soar, they're up to four,
How did they score, winning this war,
My dinks are off, no punch, no pop.

We must regroup, and close the loop,
It's time to swoop, I shout a whoop,
Partner punches, misses the drop.

Now they have five, we're still alive,
I hit a drive, it takes a dive,
My cohort gives a distant gaze.

We have a chance to win this dance,
To take a stance, to stop the trance,
We fumble with the score ablaze.

Could they have eight, it's getting late,
We don't hit straight, is this our fate,
Paddles go down for a time-out.

We dig so deep, we seem asleep,
We want to weep, the blanking bleep,
Will we ever overcome the drought?

Oh no it's ten, they serve again,
We can't pretend, to win with zen,
Our combatants are all tickled.

We lose the game, no one to blame,
We played so lame, we won't disclaim,
The humble truth, we got pickled!

Third Shot Drop

Like holding a baby chick,
Palm with a loosened grip,
Tossing up, a light flick,
Crossing net, ball will dip.

Ball bounces once within the kitchen,
The chance for points will now enrichen.

But keep in mind, my pickleball friend,
Be ready to repeat this again.

And again, and again.

Hydration

We're sweating, they're sweating,
The match is very close,
We choose to call time-out,
We need to drink fructose.

We need to drink a lot of juice,
Electrolytes will do,
We chug it down to stay footloose
Before we go askew.

We're gasping, they're gasping,
We get back on the court,
They only drank a pint,
I know we drank a quart.

All this liquid will keep me whole
Like light bulbs are to lamps,
Without the salt it takes its toll,
And I get such bad cramps.

Painfully Patient

Painfully patient.
Dink me 5, starting new climb,
Dink me 6, focusing time.

Waiting, ball drops, my backhand punches, flops,
Knuckles first, shoulders loose, push it angled, stops.

Painfully patient.
Dink me 7, watch ascent,
Dink me 8, careful descent.

Breathing, ball curves,
My forehand contacts, swerves,
Eyes on ball, compact swing,
Follow through now, nerves.

Painfully patient.
Dink me 9, oh, so sporty,
Dink me 10, final sortie.

Stalking, see spot, paddle smashes, hot,
Watching flight, body shot, saying sorry, not!

It Just Makes Me Happy

Q: Why do you play pickleball?
A: It just makes me happy.

Q: Don't you like the competition,
to win, to beat the other team?
A: It just makes me happy.

Q: Don't you feel great satisfaction mastering a
backhand dink?
A: It just makes me happy.

Q: Don't you love the exercise,
the sweat, the heart pounding?
A: It just makes me happy.

Q: Don't you love smashing the ball down
the middle splitting your opponent's paddles?
A: It just makes me happy.

Q: Don't you love winning 11-9 or 12-10
in a tough match?
A: It just makes me happy.

Q: Don't you just burst with joy coming from
behind by 7 points and winning?
A: Really. Playing pickleball just makes me happy.
See you tomorrow?

New Paddle

New paddle, grit on core,
Could I ask for anything more?

New paddle, serves go deep,
Returns are short, I win a heap.

New paddle, hardly think,
I'm master of the crosscourt dink.

New paddle, I don't fret,
They hit so hard, and I reset.

New paddle, I can shine,
Ball drives smartly right down the line.

New paddle, watch me shred,
The hard truth is it's in my head.

The Poach

Knees slightly bent, instincts afire,
If ball arcs high, don't let it bounce.

Paddle in front, I am their sire,
I start to fly, smash as I pounce.

Ball swiftly moves, I create mire,
I am not shy, a complete trounce!

A Good Leave

A good eye means a real good leave,
The shot went out, no need to try.

A good leave means you won't bereave
Next time you let a shot go by.

A good leave means they can't deceive
The ball is driven shoulder high.

A bad leave means you're quite naïve
Your blank gaze is fixed in the sky.

A bad leave means a swing pet peeve,
You know the point has gone bye-bye.

The Jerk

I should have hit the ball where?
I should have hit the ball there?

I should have gotten to the net?
I should have hit a reset?

You can't believe that I hit what?
You can't conceive we're in a rut?

I'm holding the paddle too loose?
I'm slow like a stranded caboose?

My backhand is so weak?
My forehand is so meek?

I should have covered me?
I should have taken the middle?

Why don't you see what I see?
Why not help me solve the riddle?

Just so you know, you make me irk.
Really, you are such a big jerk.

The Referee

Judge, umpire,
Adjudicator.

Don't serve before score,
Point commentator.

Ref, linesman,
One arbitrator.

Elf toes over line,
Last word debater.

Fair, honest,
Frank annotator.

Knows the rules,
Collaborator.

Too Good!

It's all those things,
Precision swings.

Super fast hits,
Perfect placed flits.

Strategic shots,
Split all the slots.

We clap in awe,
With open jaw.

We all conclude,
That shot! Too good!

Windy Day

Windy day, windy court,
Hit against, ball falls short.

With the wind, we're on guard,
Punch the ball, don't hit hard.

Crosswind builds, level fight,
Each can win, left or right.

Must relax, can't be tense,
Ball can fly, over fence.

That Shot Was Out!

That shot was out!
That shot was in.
Missed by this much.
Oh, what a sin.

Just missed the line.
What's with his eyes?
Almost did touch.
Who are these guys?

That shot was out!
This the same game?
I am the judge.
It's such a shame.

We want this bad.
They seem to cheat.
We will not budge.
We won't be beat.

Quiet Heart

Breathe,
High lob to me.

Breathe,
Think middle.

Breathe,
Think hit 100%.

Breathe,
Swing 80%.

Breathe,
Follow through.

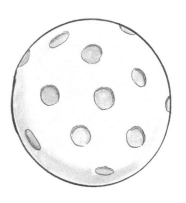

Breathe,
The lob is returned.

Breathe,
Watch your toes.

Breathe,
The lob is returned again.

Breathe,
Hit firmly down the middle.

Breathe,
They miss.

Breathe,
Smile to self.

Breathe,
Quiet heart.

Reset

Here it comes,
Third shot drive
Powers across the net.

Hold paddle
Three of five,
So easy to reset.

Fifth shot bang,
Back again,
Blasted like a rocket.

That song sang,
Know it well,
I just need to block it.

She Hears the TV Clicking

She hears the TV clicking,
A quick, consistent sound,
It's like a wristwatch ticking,
To her, it might confound.

"Who is shouting those numbers?
Why shout them out in threes?
My reading it encumbers,
I need this noise to cease."

Tournament

Pre (Awaiting)
Heart pounding, mental grounding,
Desire hounding, joy surrounding.

Match (Creating)
Heart pounding more, game we adore,
Forget the score, play with rapport.

Post (Debating)
We played to our best, and did so with zest,
We passed the tough test; we won and can rest!

Drills

We don't drill enough.
We avoid that part.
We don't like that stuff.

Yet,
Drills are at the heart
Of being more skilled.

We don't drill enough.
We don't even start.
We always rebuff.

Yet,
Drills help us outplay
The lesser self-willed.

We Play at Eight

We play at eight, please don't be late,
You may not get a court,
We hate to wait, if that's our fate,
And then you must comport.

For open play, I cannot say,
You will find your skill group,
But don't delay, it is okay,
No need to fly the coop.

Play your best game, for fun, not fame,
And do so from your lens,
Good shots and lame, there is no shame,
And you will make great friends.

The Soft Game

Play the soft game, play it real hard.

Dink your heart out, withhold your card.
Dink so careful, stay in your yard.
Dink to reset, always on guard.

Play the soft game, paddle, push, kiss.

Dink with intent, make it your bliss.
Dink very deep, slow the abyss.
Dink very short, make them submiss.

Play the soft game, play til they miss.

Court Open!

Why are they sitting there?
We just wait! Don't they care?
Don't they see the court bare?
Tell that group, off your chair!

The apathy is stunning!
Start moving! Start running!
You are next! Stop shunning!
Join the fray! No sunning!

Court open! Time to play!
Off your butts! Now! Today!

There Were Only Three to Play

He wanted to play with her,
She to play with him,
But there were only three to play,
To play was looking slim.

So he called another guy,
Then she an extra gal,
But there were only three to play,
And neither had a pal.

They resolved to find a court,
Someone would jump aboard,
But there were only three to play,
And not from their accord.

So they took the court with three,
Below the blazing sun,
But there were only three to play,
They did not need the one.

Two on one and one on two,
They played with lighter boat,
Not a problem on any day,
They all enjoyed cutthroat!

My Knee Hurts

My knee hurts, my shoulder aches,
My ankle twists, goodness sakes!

Fingers swell, back with spasm,
My mood needs enthusiasm!

Elbow sprains, now bursitis,
Suffering, sore arthritis!

My palms sweat, my cap so damp,
My arch hurts, my calf with cramp!

I am okay, I will take all,
Just give me my pickleball!

Oh, This Isn't Working!

Oh, this isn't working!
My paddle isn't straight, we're down by eight,
My partner isn't great, and I just ate
A fifth shot drive!

Oh, this isn't working!
My game is amuck, I'm half of the suck,
Running out of luck, we need to pluck
And we're barely alive!

Oh, this isn't working!
New paddle, no touch, looking for a crutch,
Rushing to net, not much, no good in the clutch,
Dink not working today!

Oh, this isn't working!
Toes over line, not a good sign,
I just can't whine, his shot, not mine,
Feels like more work than play.

Traffic Cop

The third shot drop, the traffic cop,
Sets up your fifth, so you won't flop.

Shoulder hinge toss, shape with an arc,
Don't let them drive, make your shot park.

The third shot drop, will make you think,
What to expect and where to dink.

Paddle push here, paddle punch there,
The third shot drop, with spin and flair.

The Kitchen

Your feet might cook, if you don't look,
Elf toes will curl above the line.

Toes near the edge, keep off the ledge,
Weight is balanced, very good sign.

Then push a dink, toes on the brink,
Your feet hold still in transition.

Your toes don't move, you're in the groove,
You kept them out of the kitchen.

Hand Battle

Make no mistake.
Battles will take
Rapid eye hand.

You will move fast.
The battle will last
And only one will stand.

Hit the middle.
Country fiddle,
There is no trick.

Offense, defense.
Never pretense,
One wins at quick.

You-queen or king.
Chicken wing thing,
Just one exchange.

Conquering point.
It will anoint,
Winner, short range!

Stacking

Stacking left, stacking right,
Not knowing how brings you fright.

Stacking right, stacking left,
Strategy brings winning heft.

A fist means stay, open hand, go,
Your partner should not be slow.

One finger, subtle ruse,
Feint and hold, you confuse.

Stacking fires up the griddle,
Knowing protects the middle,

Stacking works when mind is clear,
Screw it up and you pay dear.

Serve the ball from the wrong side,
Lose the point, you want to hide,

Serve the ball from the right side,
Win the point, then turn the tide.

The Bert, The Erne

Bert and Erne are related,
A family of shots,

Bert jumps far when created,
Erne jumps in smaller slots.

Bert will cross, he is a rover,
On way to his success,

Erne waits, a dinking plover,
The height he will assess.

Bert and Erne, furtive grazing,
Opponent hits up stairs,

Both attack with one shot blazing,
Rivals left with blank stares.

ATP

Around the pole, a sight to see,
Tough shot to make, it isn't free.

Your dink went wide, there is no net,
Around the pole, the stage is set.

Ball starts to drop, like on a string,
Inch above court, then paddle swing.

The ball moves swift, well, bless my soul,
A perfect shot, around the pole.

The crowd shouts loud, and claps with glee,
Such fun to watch, the ATP!

One More Stop

Beginning, middle, end,
We all need one more stop
To append our outs.

Winning, losing, bend,
We all need one more stop
To befriend our doubts.

Loving, living, send
We all need one more stop
To commend our shouts.

And Paddle Click

A word about the truth,
We all call sportsmanship.

No need to be uncouth,
Be slow to let your inside slip.

Treat with respect, they did their best,
Good shot, good try, play fair,

What troubles you should lie to rest,
A good sport means you care.

It's just a game, you win, you lose,
Play hard, play kind, be in the thick.

Play for the love, avoid the blues,
End with a smile, and paddle click.

Books by Doug Snelson

Poetry

Laughter Includes the Word: Revealed, A Life of Poetry

Children's Books

Everybody Deserves a Hug
The Fable of the Snake Named Slim
Who's Got the Face?

Printed in the USA
CPSIA information can be obtained
at www.ICGtesting.com
CBHW060913230724
11959CB00010B/96